Aiming for Progress in
Writing and Grammar

Book 1
Second Edition

William Collins' dream of knowledge for all began with the publication of his first book in 1819. A self-educated mill worker, he not only enriched millions of lives, but also founded a flourishing publishing house. Today, staying true to this spirit, Collins books are packed with inspiration, innovation and practical expertise. They place you at the centre of a world of possibility and give you exactly what you need to explore it.

Collins. Freedom to teach.

Published by Collins
An imprint of HarperCollinsPublishers
77–85 Fulham Palace Road
Hammersmith
London
W6 8JB

Browse the complete Collins catalogue at
www.collins.co.uk

10 9 8 7 6 5 4 3 2
ISBN 978-0-00-754751-7

British Library Cataloguing in Publication Data
A Catalogue record for this publication is available from the British Library.

Commissioned by Catherine Martin
Project managed by Sonya Newland
Edited in-house by Alicia Higgins
Proofread by Kelly Davis
Designed by Joerg Hartmannsgruber
Typeset by G Brasnett, Cambridge
Cover design by Angela English
Production by Rebecca Evans
Printed and bound by Martins the Printers

With thanks to Jackie Newman.

Packaged for HarperCollins by
White-Thomson Publishing Ltd.
www.wtpub.co.uk
+44 (0) 843 208 7460

Acknowledgements
The publishers gratefully acknowledge the permissions granted to reproduce copyright material in this book. While every effort has been made to trace and contact copyright holders, where this has not been possible the publishers will be pleased to make the necessary arrangements at the first opportunity.

Extracts from *Tunnel of Terror* by Barry Hutchison. Reprinted by permission of HarperCollins Publishers Ltd ©2012 Barry Hutchinson (pp 14, 15); Extract from *Cyber Shock*. Reprinted by permission of HarperCollins Publishers Ltd ©2014 Tommy Donbavand (p 18); Extracts from *The Hobbit*. Reprinted by permission of HarperCollins Publishers Ltd *The Hobbit* © The J R R Tolkien Estate Limited 1937, 1965 (p 20); Extracts from *The Name is Kade* by Alan Gibbons. Reprinted by permission of HarperCollins Publishers Ltd ©2012 Alan Gibbons and Robbie Gibbons (pp 48, 50).

The publishers would like to thank the following for permission to reproduce pictures in these pages:

Cover image and p 1 © Mikhail Hoboton Popov/Shutterstock

(t = top, b = bottom)

p 5 Sean Donohue Photo/Shutterstock, p 6t Luciano Mortula/ Shutterstock, p 6b GPI Stock/Alamy, p 7 aniad/Shutterstock, p 8 Jag_cz/Shutterstock, p 9 Vladyslav Danilin/Shutterstock, p 10t andreiuc88/Shutterstock, p 10b Sean Donohue Photo/Shutterstock, p 11 Viorel Sima/Shutterstock, p 12 Jacek Chabraszewski/ Shutterstock, p 13 oksix/Shutterstock, pp 14, 15 Illustrations from Tunnel of Terror by Barry Hutchison Reprinted by permission of HarperCollins Publishers Ltd ©2012 Ciaran Duffy, Barry Hutchinson, p 17 Paul Ridsdale Pictures/Alamy, p 18 Cover and illustrations from Cyber Shock Reprinted by permission of HarperCollins Publishers Ltd ©2014 Nic Brennan and Tommy Donbavand, p 19 Nadezhda V. Kulagina/Shutterstock, p 20 Moviestore collection Ltd/Alamy, p 21 Cover from The Hobbit Reprinted by permission of HarperCollins Publishers Ld The Hobbit © The J R R Tolkien Estate Limited 1937, 1965, p 22 Paul Ridsdale Pictures/Alamy, p 23 David Joyner/Getty Images, p 25 Nicholas Piccillo/Alamy, p 26 Mrsiraphol/Shutterstock, p 27 Paul Matzner/Alamy, p 28 Tatiana Popova /Shutterstock, p 29t natrot/Shutterstock, p 29b Kuttelvaserova Stuchelova/Shutterstock, p 30t nmedia/Shutterstock, p 30b xpixel/Shuttesrtock, p 31 vovan/ Shutterstock, p 33 Anna Omelchenko/Shutterstock, p 34t PCN Photography/Alamy, p 34b Getty Images, p 35 Kuttelvaserova Stuchelova/Shutterstock, p 36t Andresr/Shutterstock, p 36b ALLSTAR Picture Library/Alamy, p 37l Ammit Jack/Shutterstock, p 37m Greg Epperson/Shutterstock, p 37r Germanskydiver /Shutterstock, p 38 Matthew Cole/Shutterstock, p 39 Anna Omelchenko/Shutterstock, p 41 diversepixel/Shutterstock, p 42t DNF Style/Shutterstock, p 42m Chris Howey/Shutterstock, p 43 Gelpi JM/Shutterstock, p 44t Targn Pleiades/Shutterstock, p 44b Menno Schaefer/Shutterstock, p 45 IrinaK/Shutterstock, p 46 irin-k/Shutterstock, p 47 davemhunt-photography/Shutterstock, pp 48–50 Illustrations from The Name is Kade by Eoin Convenay, Alan Gibbons, Reprinted by permission of HarperCollins Publishers Ltd ©2012 Alan Gibbons and Robbie Gibbons, p 48b National Geographic Image Collection/Alamy, p 51 Rido/Shutterstock, p 53 makeitdouble/Shutterstock, p 54 diverse-pixel/Shutterstock, p 55 Getty Images, p 56t Jaren Jai Wicklund/ Shutterstock, p 56b Pressmaster/Shutterstock, p 59 AFP/Getty Images, p 60 FilmMagic/Getty Images, p 61 Wirelmage/Getty Images, p 62 Getty Images, p 63 Getty Images, p 64 MANDY GODBEHEAR/Shutterstock, p 65 oliveromg/Shutterstock, p 67 SNEHIT/Shutterstock, p 68 Victoria Kisel/Shutterstock, p 69 Franck Boston/Shutterstock, p 70t Andrew Park/Shutterstock, p 70b Ivonne Wierink/Shutterstock, p 71 Ana Gram/Shutterstock, p 73t National Geographic/Getty Images, p 73b gdvcom/Shutterstock, p 74 Warren Goldswain/Shutterstock, p 75 Irina Zolina/Shutterstock.

Contents

Chapter 1

Write with technical accuracy of syntax and punctuation in phrases, clauses and sentences

What's it all about?

You will be able to write using sentences.

In this chapter you will learn how to

- use capital letters
- explain what a sentence is and understand how to use sentences
- use full stops, question marks and exclamation marks
- use commas in lists
- recognise speech in stories.

Use capital letters

Getting you thinking

As you know, sentences need to start with a capital letter.

Capital letters must also be used to begin a person's name.

> **Examples**: Oliver, Aisha.

Capital letters are also used for place names.

> **Examples**: Australia, London, Colchester.

Capital letters must also be used for

- the days of the week: for example, Sunday
- the months of the year: for example, May
- names of events: for example, New Year's Day.

1 Look at the sentence below. Are all the capital letters in the right places? Explain why, or why not.

> the Football match was played in october.

How does it work?

Without capital letters, it is hard to work out what is being written.

2 Copy out these sentences and put capital letters in the right places.

a) my brother joe is taller than me.

b) this christmas will be a fun time.

c) christina and joanne are friends.

d) we travelled from pembroke to coventry on tuesday.

Apply your skills

3 Look at the text below. The writer was in a hurry and he has not used capital letters in his sentences. Read through his writing and decide where to put the missing capital letters.

> they wanted to steal the key. he must hide the key and escape to manchester. he'd catch an aeroplane to new zealand where he'd meet dave groves. dave would find him a safe house and he could stay there until october or november.

Check your progress

Good progress 〉〉〉

I can sometimes use capital letters correctly.

Excellent progress 〉〉〉

I use capital letters correctly most of the time.

Explain what a sentence is and understand how to use sentences

Getting you thinking

Remember, a sentence is a group of words that make sense. To make sense, a sentence needs a subject (someone or something who is doing something) and a verb (an action).

Example: Lord Lazybones laughed.

— subject
— verb

Some sentences also need an object to make sense.

Example: Lord Lazybones untied his shoelaces.

— subject
— verb
— object

Look at the three sentences below:

> **A** Lord Lazybones would never polish his shoes.
>
> **B** Mrs Snob into a cowpat.
>
> **C** scored a goal.

1 Which two sentences do not make sense? What's missing?

How does it work?

The first sentence makes sense. It has a subject, a verb and an object.

The second sentence does not make sense because it needs a verb.

Example: Mrs Snob fell into a cowpat.

You might have thought of other verbs, such as jumped or slipped.

The third sentence does not make sense because it needs a subject.

Example: Sam scored a goal.

Now you try it

2 Copy out the sentences below. Tick the sentences that make sense and complete the sentences that do not make sense.

Put the letters S, V and O above each sentence to show whether the word or phrase is the subject, verb or object:

      S   V   O

Lord Lazybones untied his shoelaces.

a) My dad his car.

b) I saw a ghost.

c) The sun shines.

d) The sun shines on my.

e) The animal growled.

f) He dug his.

g) They found gold.

Apply your skills

3 Write four sentences of your own about hobbies that you do or would like to try.

Put an S over the subject and a V over the verb. Put an O over the object if you have used one.

Check your progress

Good progress 》》

I can recognise a subject, verb and object in a sentence.

Excellent progress 》》》

I can use a subject, verb and object in a sentence.

Use full stops, question marks and exclamation marks

1 Look at the text below.

Add a full stop (**.**), question mark (**?**)

or exclamation mark (**!**) to the end of

each sentence.

> The moon was bright The man
> was hiding in the forest What was
> that noise A wolf was howling Was
> the man frightened Yes, he was
> terrified

How does it work?

Full stops are used at the end of a sentence, unless the sentence is a question (?) or an exclamation (!).

Exclamation marks are used for commands and to show strong feeling.

Examples: Come here!
Do you understand this work?
That is good. I am glad you do!

2 Look at the sentences below. Which two have the correct punctuation? Correct the two that do not.

   a) Do you think it will snow today.

   b) Hey, you!

   c) Stop at once?

   d) Have you seen the wolf?

Apply your skills

3 Copy out these sentences and end them with a full stop, exclamation mark or question mark.

   a) Watch out

   b) How many cats have you got

   c) It was a cold day

4 Now write four sentences of your own. Write about your pets or an animal you have known.

Use at least one full stop, one exclamation mark and one question mark.

Ask a partner to check your work.

Check your progress

Good progress

I understand when to use full stops, exclamation marks and question marks.

Excellent progress 》》》

I can write using full stops, exclamation marks and question marks correctly.

Use commas in lists

Getting you thinking

This is a comma (**,**). It is used to break up lists of words.

> **Example**: In my bag I put a pen, pencil, ruler, t-shirt and trainers.

1 Copy out the following sentence and put commas in the right places.

> My favourite sports are cycling swimming cricket and basketball.

How does it work?

You use the word 'and' instead of a comma before the final item in a list.

Now you try it

2 Look at the sentences below. Which two have the correct punctuation? Correct the two that do not.

a) I bought chocolate milk eggs bread and a cereal bar from the shop.

b) My pets are a dog, a cat, a hamster and three goldfish.

c) Arsenal, Liverpool, Spurs and Chelsea have bought new players this season.

d) We will meet Nihal Jason Suzie and Chrissie outside the cinema.

3 Write a sentence using each of these groups of words. Make sure you use commas.

a) apples pears peaches grapes plums

b) history English geography French maths

c) lion tiger elephant kangaroo monkey.

4 Write a sentence of your own that includes a list. Make it about your favourite sport or a sport you enjoy watching.

Remember to use commas and ask a partner to check it for you.

Check your progress

Good progress 〉〉

I understand that commas are used in lists.

Excellent progress 〉〉〉

I can use commas to break up lists.

Recognise speech in stories

Getting you thinking

In *Tunnel of Terror* Jim and Karl are riding a ghost train at midnight. Something seems to be wrong:

> Another door opened at the other end of the platform. A car shot through and stopped right in front of Jim and Karl.
>
> 'It's empty,' Jim said.
>
> 'Yeah, so?'
>
> 'Well ... where did the people go? Isn't this the only way off and on?'
>
> Karl shrugged. 'They probably got off somewhere else.' He jumped down into the car. 'Now come on, let's get this over with.'

1 What do you notice about how the speech is set out in the example above? Discuss your ideas with a partner.

How does it work?

If speech is set out correctly, it makes it easier to understand when people are speaking.

Whenever someone speaks in a story, the writer starts a new line. The writer puts speech marks ('...') around what that person says.

2 Jim and Karl are now in the ghost train. They have just passed some skeletons. Put in speech marks where you think people are actually speaking.

They were pretty good, Jim admitted, as the light went out again. They looked almost real.

Another scream echoed along the dark passageway. This time both boys jumped.

That one sounded better, Karl said.

Yeah, Jim nodded, and a cold breeze tickled his neck. They sounded really scared, didn't they?

Karl didn't answer. The only sound in the tunnel was the creaking of the car along the track.

Don't you think? Jim said.

Karl still didn't answer.

Karl?

Tunnel of Terror by Barry Hutchison

Apply your skills

3 Imagine Jim realises that Karl isn't sitting next to him. Instead it is a stranger. Karl has disappeared. Think carefully about what Jim and the stranger might say to each other. Write three or four sentences using speech marks.

Check your progress
....

Good progress 〉〉

I understand that a writer uses a new line for speech in stories as well as speech marks.

Excellent progress 〉〉〉

I can write and correctly set out speech in stories.

Check your progress

Good progress

- [ ] I can sometimes use capital letters correctly.
- [ ] I can recognise a subject, verb and object in a sentence.
- [ ] I understand when to use full stops, exclamation marks and question marks.
- [ ] I understand that commas are used in lists.
- [ ] I understand that a writer uses a new line for speech in stories as well as speech marks.

Excellent progress

- [ ] I use capital letters correctly most of the time.
- [ ] I can use a subject, verb and object in a sentence.
- [ ] I can use commas to break up lists.
- [ ] I can write using full stops, exclamation marks and question marks correctly.
- [ ] I can write and correctly set out speech in stories.

Chapter 2

Vary sentences for clarity, purpose and effect

What's it all about?

You will be able to use a range of sentences to interest your reader.

In this chapter you will learn how to

- recognise the present and the past tense in stories
- switch between the present and the past tense
- join sentences together using conjunctions.

Recognise the present and the past tense in stories

Getting you thinking

Look at the example below taken from a story called *Cyber Shock*. Mark is tackled in a game of football. He's hurt.

> His trousers were torn, and I expected to see loads of blood where he'd cut himself – but there was none of that. Mark's skin was ripped back and, inside his knee, there was a long, metal bar and loads of coloured wires. There was even a tiny circuit board, like the one you get in computers.
>
> *Cyber Shock* by Tommy Donbavand

1 Is the example above written in the present or the past tense? Discuss your ideas with a partner.

How does it work?

Some stories are written in the present tense. They use verb forms such as 'is', 'are' and 'look'.

Some stories are written in the past tense. They use verb forms such as 'was', 'were' and 'looked'.

2 a) Write about something that happened to you yesterday. Use just three or four sentences and write in the past tense.

b) With a partner, underline the words in your writing that show it is in the past tense.

Apply your skills

Here is another story. This one is written in the present, as if it is happening now:

> I can see the boy in black. He's ugly and big and scary. He's the leader of the gang. I've got to avoid him ... somehow. I hear a noise and turn quickly. Other members of the gang are behind me. I'm trapped!

3 Which words tell you that the story is about something that is happening now?

4 Write four or five sentences in the present tense about somebody who is facing danger.

Check your progress

Good progress 〉〉〉
I can recognise the past and the present tense in stories.

Excellent progress 〉〉〉
I can write using the past and the present tense.

Switch between the present and the past tense

Getting you thinking

Read this text from *The Hobbit*:

> Deep down here by the dark water lived old Gollum, a small slimy creature. I don't know where he came from, nor who or what he was. He was Gollum – as dark as darkness, except for two big round pale eyes in his thin face.
>
> *The Hobbit* by J. R. R. Tolkien

1 What tense do you think the text is written in? Write down any words that tell you it is written in that tense.

How does it work?

The text is written in the past tense because it uses words such as 'lived' and 'was'.

Now you try it

2 Rewrite the text from *The Hobbit* in the present tense. Underline the words you have changed.

Apply your skills

3 Write a paragraph of your own in the present tense. You could base it on *The Hobbit* or another story you know well.

4 Now rewrite your paragraph in the past tense.

5 Get into groups of seven or eight. Six people should form a tunnel. The other one or two should slowly walk through the tunnel.

Each person forming the tunnel must whisper a word in the past tense as the person walks through. Those going through the tunnel should change the word into the present tense.

Once someone has walked through, they join the tunnel and someone else walks through.

Check your progress

Good progress 〉〉
I can change the present to the past tense.

Excellent progress 〉〉〉
I can move from the present to the past tense and back again, and recognise how my writing has changed.

Join sentences together using conjunctions

Getting you thinking

Short sentences can be joined together to make longer sentences. You can do this by adding (and), (but), (so) or (because). These are examples of *conjunctions*.

Example 1:
Jim was ill. He saw the doctor.
Jim was ill so he saw the doctor.

Example 2:
A car skidded. The road was icy.
A car skidded because the road was icy.

1 Which conjunction could you use to join these two sentences together?

> I was looking forward to the film.
> The cinema was closed.

How does it work?

By using conjunctions you can turn two small sentences into one longer sentence.

Now you try it

2 Join these sentences together with 'and', 'but', 'so' or 'because':

a) Ali was tired. He had cycled a long way.

b) It was hot. We went to the beach.

c) The forest fire was fierce. The firefighters put it out.

d) Amy liked music. She bought a new CD.

3 Here is a paragraph. Fill in the spaces with a suitable conjunction.

> We were on holiday _____ we decided to explore the village. It was near the sea _____ we promised mum we wouldn't go there alone. We decided to walk around the village _____ it looked interesting. Soon we felt hungry _____ we found the local fish and chip shop.

Check your progress

Good progress 》

I understand that conjunctions can be used to join sentences.

Excellent progress 》》

I can use the conjunctions 'and', 'but', 'so' or 'because' to join sentences.

Check your progress

Good progress

☐ I can recognise the past and the present tense in stories.

☐ I can change the present to the past tense.

☐ I understand that conjunctions can be used to join sentences.

Excellent progress

☐ I can write using the past and the present tense.

☐ I can move from the present to the past tense and back again, and recognise how my writing has changed.

☐ I can use the conjunctions 'and', 'but', 'so' or 'because' to join sentences.

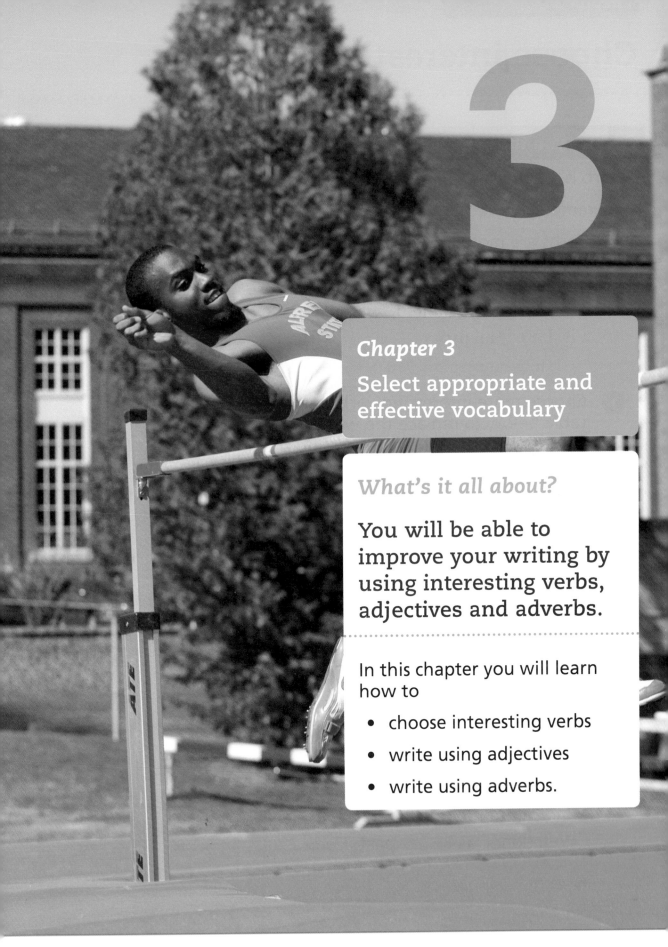

3

Chapter 3
Select appropriate and effective vocabulary

What's it all about?

You will be able to improve your writing by using interesting verbs, adjectives and adverbs.

In this chapter you will learn how to

- choose interesting verbs
- write using adjectives
- write using adverbs.

Choose interesting verbs

Getting you thinking

A verb is a doing or being word.

Examples: I am, she runs

Some verbs are more interesting than others.
Look at these sentences:

> I saw a cake on the table. I ran over and
> took it. I ate it all up!

1 Choose more interesting verbs from the table below to replace the words in red. Rewrite the sentences above using the more interesting verbs.

gobbled	looked at	snatched	chewed
noticed	dashed	grabbed	raced

How does it work?

Using interesting verbs will improve your work and make it livelier.

Now you try it

Look at the sentences below:

> It was sports day. I tried the high jump
> and ran around the track. My friend Alex
> said 'Well done!' as I went past. I walked
> to the refreshment tent and got a drink.

2 Replace the verbs in red with more interesting verbs of your own choice.

Apply your skills

3 **a)** Write a few sentences about a sports day you remember. Make sure you include some interesting verbs.

b) Working with a partner, try to improve each other's verbs.

Check your progress
....

Good progress 》》

I can recognise and use some interesting verbs in my writing.

Excellent progress 》》》

I can use a variety of interesting verbs in my writing.

Write using adjectives

Getting you thinking

Look at the text below:

It was a Monday morning. Mum drove me to school in our car. Mr Fothergill was waiting outside the classroom. Then I realised I wasn't wearing my school uniform. I was still dressed in my pyjamas!

1 Discuss with a partner how the text could be made more interesting.

Now here are the first two sentences of the text with adjectives added:

It was a dark, cloudy Monday morning. Mum drove me to school in our little blue car.

2 With your partner, come up with some adjectives you could add to the other sentences in the text.

How does it work?

Using adjectives makes your sentences more interesting. For example, the adjectives 'dark' and 'cloudy' tell your reader about the weather that morning.

3 Add some adjectives to the following text:

> There was a _____ lorry outside Mr Hill's _____ garage. Men were loading a _____ car onto the van. One man was dressed in an _____, _____ coat. A _____ dog snapped at his _____ feet. I knew _____ Mr Hill would never allow this _____ man near his garage.

Apply your skills

4 Look at the following sentences. Replace the adjectives in red with more interesting ones. Use a thesaurus to help you.

a) The boy felt cross.

b) Amelia's birthday present was a small puppy.

c) It was raining so Zack was wet.

d) The frightened mouse hid in the corner.

e) My gran was happy when I gave her the flowers.

Check your progress
....

Good progress 》》

I can use adjectives to make my writing more interesting.

Excellent progress 》》》

I can use a thesaurus to find alternative adjectives to improve my writing.

Write using adverbs

Getting you thinking

An adverb is a word that tells us more about a verb or adjective. Adverbs often answer the question: 'How?' Many adverbs end in 'ly' or 'ily'.

Examples: The teacher spoke loudly.
The girl laughed happily.

1 Add a suitable adverb to the following. Choose words that end in 'ly'.

a) The snail moved _____.

b) The girl whispered _____.

c) The boys ran _____.

How does it work?

Adjectives describe nouns.

Example: The slow tortoise.

You can change many adjectives into adverbs by adding 'ly'. Adverbs give more information about a verb – they describe how an action is performed.

Example: The tortoise crawled slowly.

2 Change these four adjectives into adverbs by adding 'ly'. Then write a sentence for each one.

a) dear

b) clever

c) smooth

d) rude.

3 Look at the three sentences below and add an adverb that ends in 'ly'.

a) He swam _____.

b) She _____ lost her temper.

c) She spoke _____ to her puppy.

Apply your skills

To change an adjective that ends in a 'y' to an adverb, you need to change the 'y' to an 'i' before adding 'ly'.

Example: 'heavy' becomes 'heavily'.

4 Change these adjectives into adverbs.

a) hasty

b) icy

c) handy.

Check your progress

Good progress 》》

I can use adverbs in my writing.

Excellent progress 》》

I can spell adverbs that end in 'ly' and 'ily' and use them in my writing.

Check your progress

Good progress

- [ ] I can recognise and use some interesting verbs in my writing.
- [ ] I can use adjectives to make my writing more interesting.
- [ ] I can use adverbs in my writing.

Excellent progress

- [ ] I can use a variety of interesting verbs in my writing.
- [ ] I can use a thesaurus to find alternative adjectives to improve my writing.
- [ ] I can spell adverbs that end in 'ly' and 'ily' and use them in my writing.

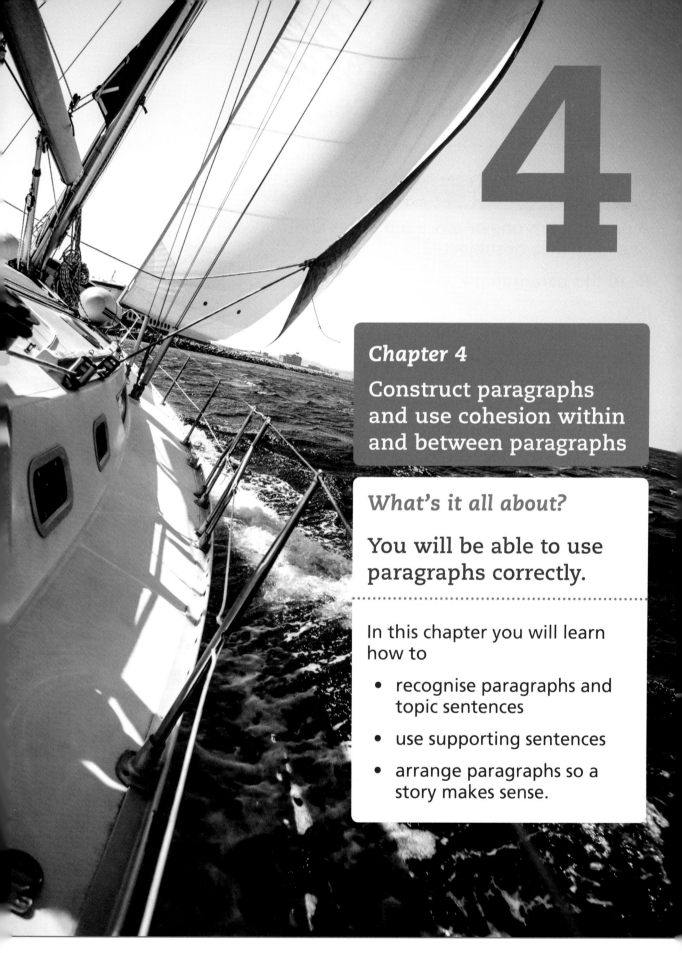

4

Chapter 4
Construct paragraphs and use cohesion within and between paragraphs

What's it all about?

You will be able to use paragraphs correctly.

In this chapter you will learn how to

- recognise paragraphs and topic sentences
- use supporting sentences
- arrange paragraphs so a story makes sense.

Recognise paragraphs and topic sentences

Getting you thinking

A paragraph is one or more sentences about one main idea or subject.

Read this paragraph:

> The biggest motor race in the USA is the Indianapolis 500, usually called the 'Indy 500'. It is held during the last weekend of May. The drivers race 500 miles, which is 200 times round the track. It is even more dangerous than Formula One. There are more cars in the race. The track is a lot shorter.

1 With a partner, decide which is the most important sentence in the paragraph.

How does it work?

Writers start a new paragraph to show that they are going to write about a new idea or subject.

The most important sentence in a paragraph is called the *topic sentence*.

In the example above, the first sentence is the topic sentence. The sentences that follow tell us more about the Indy 500.

Read this paragraph:

> Jamie Duff needed glasses. He kicked a ball. But the ball was a hard, round stone! Jamie's toes hurt. His friends laughed.

2 a) What is this paragraph about?

b) What is the topic sentence in this paragraph?

Apply your skills

3 Sometimes, the most important sentence does not come first. Which is the topic sentence in the paragraph below?

> Teachers were frightened. Rats had invaded the school. They crawled on to the dinner plates. They chewed food in the kitchen. They crawled into the head teacher's hair.

4 a) Write a paragraph of four or five sentences about Mr Green, who saw mini-beasts invade his garden. Which do you think is your topic sentence?

b) When you have finished, check through your work with a partner. Can your partner identify the topic sentence?

Check your progress

Good progress 》》
I can recognise a paragraph and its topic sentence.

Excellent progress 》》》
I can write a paragraph that includes a topic sentence.

Use supporting sentences

Getting you thinking

The topic sentence is the main sentence in a paragraph. The other sentences in a paragraph are called supporting sentences.

Read this paragraph:

> Angie wanted to be good at tennis. She practised every day. She hit the ball against a wall. She watched videos about her favourite players. Her younger sister still beat her every time.

1 Which sentences do you think are the supporting sentences?

How does it work?

Supporting sentences give you more detail about the topic.

Now you try it

2 Pick out the topic sentence and four supporting sentences from the paragraph below:

> Tiger Woods is one of the greatest golfers ever known. He wanted to play golf early on in his life.

He played against a champion when he was only six years old and he lost by just one stroke. He has gone on to win 79 official tour events and 14 major titles. He holds many records and he's still playing!

Apply your skills

Look at these three pictures:

3 Write a paragraph about what is happening in each of the pictures. Use a topic sentence and three supporting sentences for each picture.

Check your progress

Good progress >>>
I can recognise the supporting sentences in a paragraph.

Excellent progress >>>
I can write a paragraph using a topic sentence and supporting sentences.

Arrange paragraphs so a story makes sense

Getting you thinking

The paragraphs in the story below are all jumbled up:

Cousin Mike

A One day, I found a room full of really big hairy spiders. I took the spiders and put them in a box. I put the box through Cousin Mike's letterbox.

B If a child fell over in the park, Mike would laugh. If a child cried, he would laugh even more. If a child had a fever he would laugh until he cried.

C I heard Mike scream. He ran out of the house and down the road. Nobody saw him again.

D Cousin Mike was a horror. He hated spiders and he hated having a good time. He hated watching television. He hated watching sport. Most of all, he hated children.

1 Working in pairs, see if you can work out the correct order for the paragraphs.

How does it work?

Putting the paragraphs in order means the story will make sense.

2 Read 'Cousin Mike' again with the paragraphs in the right order. Then answer these questions:

　　a) Which is the topic sentence in each paragraph?

　　b) What is each paragraph about?

　　c) How does the order of the paragraphs help you make sense of the story?

Apply your skills

Here is a story about a shipwreck:

We had decided to sail across the Atlantic Ocean. We set off from New York. We wanted to reach the west coast of England. We were doing fine until a storm hit us. This was the worst storm we'd ever seen. The wind rocked our tiny boat. We decided to get below deck. We didn't want anyone swept overboard. A big wave flipped our boat over. We were trapped inside our cabin. We were upside down. It was getting difficult to breathe. We didn't want to die.

3 The story is made up of three paragraphs. Where do you think each new paragraph should start?

4 Complete the story about a shipwreck by writing a paragraph of your own.

Check your progress

Good progress 》》

I can order paragraphs so a story makes sense.

Excellent progress 》》

I can order paragraphs and understand where a new paragraph is needed.

Check your progress

Good progress

☐ I can recognise a paragraph and its topic sentence.

☐ I can recognise supporting sentences in a paragraph.

☐ I can order paragraphs so a story makes sense.

Excellent progress

☐ I can write a paragraph that includes a topic sentence.

☐ I can write a paragraph using a topic sentence and supporting sentences.

☐ I can order paragraphs and understand where a new paragraph is needed.

5

Chapter 5

Organise and present whole texts effectively, sequencing and structuring information, ideas and events

What's it all about?

You will be able to organise your ideas for writing.

In this chapter you will learn how to

- plan your writing
- use bullet points and headings
- write the opening of a story
- continue your story by describing and then solving the problem.

Plan your writing

Before you do any type of writing, it is a good idea to have a plan. One way you can do this is by making a flow chart. You will need to think of key headings and put them in a logical order. Then summarise your ideas under each heading.

Example: Anita is going to give a speech about puppies and dogs. She plans her speech by making a flow chart.

Opening
Why I wanted a puppy.

Choosing the right puppy
Friendly, bright eyes. Looks healthy.

Routine
Feeding/cleaning/ bedtimes.

House training
Affection – not too much.
Toilet training.
Playing with toys, not chewing furniture or doors.

Visiting the vet
Check health.
Injections.

Puppy training
Walking on a lead.
Acting properly around other dogs and people.

Problem dogs
Rescue dogs, vicious dogs and how to cure bad behaviour.

1 Do you think Anita has made a good plan for her speech? Why, or why not?

How does it work?

A good plan shows you the order of your speech (or any piece of writing) and gives an idea of what you will cover in each section.

Now you try it

2 a) Think of a subject you are interested in. You might want to use a spider diagram to note down some ideas.

b) Then turn some of those ideas into a flow chart by setting out headings and writing a few notes under each heading.

Apply your skills

3 Use your plan to write a speech about the subject you have chosen. Each heading is like a new paragraph.

4 Learn your speech by heart, rehearsing it with a partner. Then give your speech in front of your group or class.

Check your progress

Good progress 》》

I understand how a plan can help organise my writing.

Excellent progress 》》

I can draw up a plan and use it to organise my writing effectively.

Use bullet points and headings

Read the text below about the red squirrel:

The red squirrel is the only squirrel native to Britain. It has struggled to survive since the grey squirrel was introduced to Britain from America. Red squirrels eat seeds and pine cones. They also eat fruits from shrubs and trees. They sometimes eat birds' eggs. Holding nuts in their paws, red squirrels are able to recognise good nuts and bad nuts. They only eat the best nuts!

Organise and present whole texts effectively, sequencing and structuring information

Now read the text about the grey squirrel:

The Grey Squirrel

- Not all grey squirrels are grey. A few are black or yellow.

- Black squirrels have been spotted in parts of England.

- Grey squirrel babies are called kittens.

- Kittens are born with their eyes closed and without any teeth or hair.

- Grey squirrels can swim.

1 Which text is easier to read? Why?

How does it work?

The information about the grey squirrel includes a clear heading and bullet points. It is easier to read. You can find information about the animal quickly.

You are going to write about an insect or animal that interests you.

2 a) Use the internet or read library books to find out more about your chosen insect or animal.

b) Decide what your main headings will be. For example, 'Where it lives', 'What it eats' or 'Amazing facts'.

c) Write three or four bullet points for each heading.

Apply your skills

You are now going to write a fact sheet about your insect or animal. Look at this example fact sheet about wildcats.

Wildcat fact sheet

Description

The wildcat looks like a strong tabby cat. Its coat is brown with black stripes or spots. Wildcats walk like lions and they have thick bushy tails.

Where wildcats live and hunt

Wildcats mostly live and hunt in Highland forests in Scotland. They usually hunt alone. They mark out their area by leaving a scent (a smell).

Home life

Wildcat kittens are born in a nest called a den. They leave the den when they are a month old. Their mother teaches them to hunt very soon after they are born.

Defence

Wildcats can growl and spit. They mock-charge, pretending they are lions!

Problems

People thought wildcats were pests so they were hunted and killed. There are now only four hundred wildcats left in Scotland.

Conclusion

Wildcats are interesting because they look like pet cats. But they are different from pet cats and can never be tamed.

3 Set out your headings and write a few sentences under each heading.

When you have finished, you will have a fact sheet about your favourite insect or animal.

4 Working in pairs, read each other's fact sheets. Say how the fact sheets can be improved. Think about the following questions:

a) Has your partner used headings?

b) Is the fact sheet easy to read?

c) Does it make sense?

Top tip

Remember to use clear headings and expand your ideas into paragraphs.

Check your progress

Good progress >>>

I can use clear headings and bullet points to organise my writing.

Excellent progress >>>

I can turn bullet points into paragraphs and set out a piece of writing clearly.

Write the opening of a story

Read the two story openings below:

The Name is Kade

The name is Kade, Jack Kade. I take the jobs the cops can't do. I clear the skyways of the scum of the universe. I hunt down the gangsters, the kidnappers, every kind of low life. It's a dirty job, but somebody has to do it. I get my orders from the top.

by Alan Gibbons

The Old Sweet Shop

The old sweet shop at the corner of the street had been shut for years. One day it opened again. An old lady served behind the counter. Behind her, on the walls, were long wooden shelves. The shelves were filled with jars of sweets.

When children entered the shop, the old lady appeared. She did not speak to anyone. She just nodded when someone ordered sweets. She smelt like rotten eggs. Some said she was a ghost. But she was not a ghost – she was something *far scarier*!

1. Which opening do you like best? Discuss with a partner:

   a) Which opening makes you want to read on and find out more?

   b) What do you think the story will be about?

   c) What do you think will happen next?

How does it work?

A good opening should make the reader want to find out more. Often it will introduce the setting and the main characters.

Now you try it

2. Look back at the two extracts. Do they make you want to find out more? Do they set the scene and introduce the main characters?

Apply your skills

3. Write a short opening to a story. Call your story *The Name Is Jake* (or *Jackie*).

   Give your character a dangerous job to do and let him or her explain the job.

   Keep your sentences short and exciting. Make sure the reader will want to find out more!

Check your progress

Good progress 》》
I understand the key features of a good story opening.

Excellent progress 》》》
I can write the start of a story, introducing the key features of a good story.

Continue your story by describing and then solving the problem

Getting you thinking

Read the start of *The Name is Kade* (on page 48) again. Then read the next paragraph below. It tells you about a problem, which needs to be solved.

> So there I was at Pad 5, Saturn City. Saturn City is the hub. From there you can reach most of the known planets. I pulled out my phone and looked at the mug shot of my latest target. I had to find him and put him back in prison where he belonged.

1 Discuss the following questions with a partner:

a) Do you like the way this story has continued?

b) What new things do we find out?

How does it work?

A writer often introduces a problem in the *middle* of the story. This problem is usually solved at the end of the story.

Now you try it

2 In small groups, talk about what might happen next in the story *The Name is Kade*.

Apply your skills

3 Think of a problem that the hero or heroine in your own story might face. Briefly describe the problem.

4 Now write the end of your story. You will need to solve the problem.

5 Discuss the following questions with a partner:

a) Did they understand what the main problem was?

b) Did they understand the solution to the problem?

c) Did your story hold their interest right up to the end?

Check your progress

Good progress

I can include a problem that needs to be solved in my story.

Excellent progress

I can write an interesting story with a clear problem that is solved at the end.

Check your progress

Good progress 》》

- [ ] I understand how a plan can help organise my writing.
- [ ] I can use clear headings and bullet points to organise my writing.
- [ ] I understand the key features of a good story opening.
- [ ] I can develop a story by adding a problem that needs to be solved.

Excellent progress 》》》

- [ ] I can draw up a plan and use it to organise my writing effectively.
- [ ] I can turn bullet points into paragraphs and set out a piece of writing clearly.
- [ ] I can write the start of a story, introducing the key features of a story.
- [ ] I can write a story that includes a problem with a clear resolution by the end.

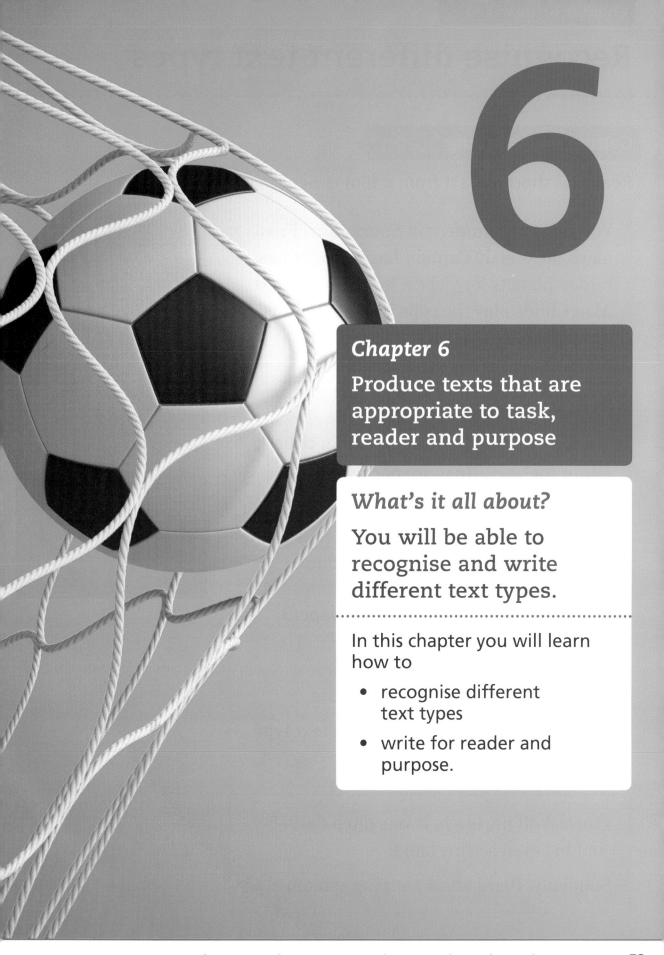

Chapter 6

Produce texts that are appropriate to task, reader and purpose

What's it all about?

You will be able to recognise and write different text types.

In this chapter you will learn how to

- recognise different text types
- write for reader and purpose.

Recognise different text types

Read this short extract from a film review:

> You must see *Raiders in Space*. Karl Frost
> plays the greedy Captain Lashor, who has
> raided planets for riches. Belle Brown and
> Alan Childs play the cops who chase him
> through space and time.

You can work out what type of text it is by
asking yourself these questions:

Who wrote it? (for example, film critic)

Who for?   (newspaper reader)

Why?   (to tell reader about film)

Here are some different text types:

- Descriptive – a story or a travel book /
  a poem / a letter to a friend.

- Informative – a diary or a newspaper /
  magazine article / business letter.

- Instructive – a manual.

- Persuasive – an advert / a brochure.

1 Look at the text below. What text type
do you think it is? Why?

> I turned off my torch. It was pitch dark. I
> couldn't even see my hand.
>
> Suddenly, there was a piercing scream...

2 With a partner, decide which text type best fits the following examples.

a) Dear Diary, today was awesome. I scored the winning goal against…

b) Dear Sir/Madam, I am writing to you because your assistant refused to change my coat, even though…

c) Travel to India! It's cheaper than you think. Our planes are fast and our hotels are…

d) Next, tighten each spoke with the small spanner provided and then…

Apply your skills

3 Write a diary entry about your favourite team scoring a winning goal. Remember:

- You are writing for yourself, not for other people.

- You should write the date at the top of your entry.

- You should describe your feelings about the goal.

4 Now write an extract from a newspaper article about the winning goal. Remember:

- You are writing for lots of other people.

- You should use a headline at the top of your article to draw readers in.

Check your progress

Good progress ⟩⟩
I can recognise the different features of various text types.

Excellent progress ⟩⟩⟩
I can recognise and write using the different features of various text types.

Write for reader and purpose

Getting you thinking

When you write, you need to think about who you are writing for (*reader*) and what you are writing for (*purpose*).

1 Imagine you are going to write a letter to your friend about a holiday you are enjoying. Jot down some notes about what you might include.

How does it work?

You need to think about who the letter is for (reader). Your writing needs to be right for that person.

You also need to think about why you are writing the letter (purpose).

Now you try it

Lissie is having a party and she wants to invite her friend. Lissie has a reader (her friend) and a purpose (persuasion).

12 Crossover Lane,
Mardley,
Worcester
W1 0LM
14th May 2014

— address goes in the right-hand corner

Dear Isabella,——— audience / reader

School is boring without you. I can't tease old Mr — paragraph one – opening
Miller about his dress sense. There's a weird new
boy who sits in your old place.

Guess what? Mum's letting me have a great big ——— paragraph two – purpose (the reason for writing)
party in the village hall. I can invite loads of people
and we'll have loud music. Can you come for a ——— makes it sound fun
sleepover at my place?

Please come: it'll be fun. Give me a call or text me.——— concluding paragraph

Love, Lissie
——— informal, as this is a letter to a friend

2 Write Isabella's reply, accepting the invitation.

Apply your skills

Isabella's mum says that Isabella can't go to the party.

3 Write another letter from Isabella to Lissie, apologising for not being able to go.

4 Write a letter from Lissie to Isabella's mum, trying to change her mind. What information would she change or leave out? What more polite or grown-up words might Lissie choose?

Check your progress

Good progress »»

I can write a letter bearing in mind my reader and purpose.

Excellent progress »»

I can write a persuasive letter appropriate to reader and purpose.

Check your progress

Good progress

☐ I can recognise the different features of various text types.

☐ I can write a letter bearing in mind my reader and purpose.

Excellent progress

☐ I can recognise and write using the different features of various text types.

☐ I can write a persuasive letter appropriate to reader and purpose.

Chapter 7

Write imaginative, interesting and thoughtful texts

What's it all about?

You will be able to make your work as interesting as possible.

In this chapter you will learn how to

- express opinions
- redraft your text to improve it.

Express opinions

Getting you thinking

Here are some people of your own age, giving their opinions about music:

I think One Direction are the best band because they sing amazing songs like 'Story of My Life'. They are a boy band based in London and they are great when they sing live.

Laura

I think Leona Lewis is the best pop singer because she can really sing, not like some pop stars. 'Glassheart' is a fantastic song and she sings it really well.

Zoe

Adele is the best singer around. Her voice is amazing. She's also a songwriter and she's a musician who can play more than one instrument. She's really talented.

Jordan

1 Which opinion do you think is expressed most clearly? Why?

How does it work?

Three students of your own age have expressed their opinions about a band or singer. They have given the reasons why they like that particular band or singer.

Now you try it

You are going to answer the question:
'Who is the music personality of the year?'

For example, you might write:

> I think Adele is the music personality of the year because she writes and sings great songs.

2 Pick a band or a singer. Use the internet to find out what they have done and make notes using bullet points.

3 Write about your music personality of the year. Make your writing interesting by using imaginative adjectives and adverbs and giving reasons.

4 In groups, take turns to read your pieces of writing. Then vote for the music personality of the year.

Add up the votes and list the three people who got the most votes.

Now vote for the best of the top three. Who has won? Who is the music personality of the year?

5 Write a few sentences explaining your own opinion of the top three.

Apply your skills

Look at these four candidates for sports person of the year:

Andy Murray (tennis player), British tennis number 1, from Glasgow

When he won the US Open in 2012, Andy became the first British male tennis player to win a Grand Slam since 1936. Winning the Wimbledon Championship in 2013 meant Britain had its first champion for 77 years.

Jessica Ennis (track athlete), heptathlon gold medal, from Sheffield

Jessica won the heptathlon at the London Olympic Games in 2012. She gained her gold medal in style, winning the last event when she only needed eighth place.

Mo Farah (long-distance runner), born in Somalia

Britain's best-ever long-distance runner. During the 2012 London Olympic Games, he won gold in the 5,000 m and the 10,000 m. He now has a gold medal for each of his twin girls!

Usain Bolt (sprinter), from Jamaica

Usain is nicknamed 'Lightning Bolt' because he's thought to be the fastest person ever! He won three gold medals during the Beijing Olympic Games and three gold medals during the London Olympic Games. He also won three golds during the 2013 Moscow World Championships.

6 Which of these athletes do you think should be sports person of the year? Write down your answer and give reasons for your choice.

Check your progress

....

Good progress 》》》

I can express opinions in my writing.

Excellent progress 》》》

I can express and give reasons for my opinions.

Redraft your text to improve it

Getting you thinking

Look at the first draft of this short piece of writing about bullying:

> I think schools should have good policies about bullying. Some schools have sixth formers who are willing to talk to students who are bullied. They then speak to the bullies.
>
> Bullies often find someone who is weaker than they are and this means that bullies are cowards. They also don't accept any blame for their behaviour.
>
> Cyber bullying is on the increase.
>
> There are lots of things you can do if you are bullied.

1 How do you think this text could be improved? For example, does it need a closing paragraph? Discuss this with a partner.

How does it work?

Much more could be written about cyber bullying and what can be done to help those who are bullied.

To improve the piece, the writer will need to redraft it. Redrafting means:

- re-reading the text
- adding more information where it is needed
- choosing or adding better words
- correcting any mistakes
- making a final draft.

Now you try it

2 Use the library or the internet to do some more research on bullying.

Make notes on the information you find.

3 Now redraft the text about bullying, using the bullet points above to help you. Remember to include a closing paragraph.

Apply your skills

4 Having written your article, go through your work with a partner to see how the piece has been improved since the first draft. Check that

- you have included enough information in each section
- your sentences make sense
- you have used paragraphs correctly
- your spelling is correct
- your writing sounds interesting.

Top tip

You might want to look up Childline's advice about bullying and about National Anti-Bullying week.

Check your progress

Good progress 》

I understand what steps I need to take to redraft my work.

Excellent progress 》》

I can write and redraft my work to improve it.

Check your progress

Good progress

- [ ] I can express opinions in my writing.
- [ ] I understand what steps I need to take to redraft my work.

Excellent progress

- [ ] I can express and give reasons for my opinions.
- [ ] I can write and redraft my work to improve it.

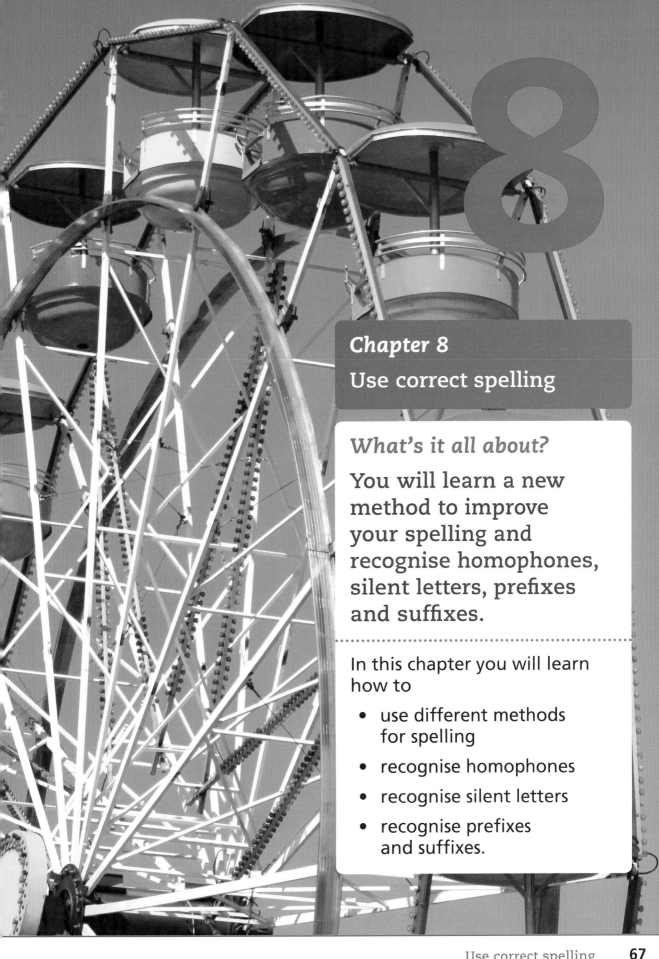

Chapter 8
Use correct spelling

What's it all about?

You will learn a new method to improve your spelling and recognise homophones, silent letters, prefixes and suffixes.

In this chapter you will learn how to

- use different methods for spelling
- recognise homophones
- recognise silent letters
- recognise prefixes and suffixes.

Use different methods for spelling

You can learn how to spell a word by using the 'look-think-say-cover-write-check' method:

1   **Look** at the word very carefully.

2   **Think** about the parts of the word that might cause problems.

3   **Say** the word out loud or in your head.

4   **Cover** the word up.

5   **Write** the word out without looking at it again.

6   **Check** to see if you have got it right.

If you have still misspelled the word, follow steps 1 to 6 again.

1   Use the method above to learn the following words:

   a) problem

   b) learn

   c) dictionary

   d) science.

2   Work with a partner to check you know the spellings. One partner reads out the words, while the other writes them down.

How does it work?

If you keep looking at the correct spelling and use the look-think-say-cover-write-check method, you can often learn to spell a word correctly.

Now you try it

3 Try spelling these words and get a partner to test you and check them:

a) sailor   b) character

c) following   d) correct

e) spelling   f) sentence

g) brother   h) burst

4 Write out any words you did not get right and use the look-think-say-cover-write-check method. Then test yourself again.

Apply your skills

You can also learn spellings by looking up words in a dictionary.

5 Work with a partner. One of you should spell out each word below. The other should find the word in a dictionary:

a) across   b) forty

c) think   d) narrator

6 Once you have found the words in a dictionary, use the look-think-say-cover-write-check method to learn the spellings thoroughly.

Check your progress

Good progress

I can use the look-think-say-cover-write-check method to learn unknown spellings.

Excellent progress

I can use the look-think-say-cover-write-check method and use a dictionary to check my spelling.

Recognise homophones

Getting you thinking

Homophones are words that sound the same but have different meanings and often different spellings.

Example: fair   fare

'I'm riding on the ferris wheel at the fair.'

'I paid my bus fare today.'

1. With a partner, use a dictionary to check the meaning of these homophones:

   a) cereal/serial   b) leak/leek

   c) beach/beech.

Now you try it

2. Copy out the sentences below using the correct homophone. Then check your answers with a partner:

   a) I saw a ball/bawl on the beach.

   b) I blew/blue on the fire.

   c) The pop banned/band played in the Town Hall.

   d) My brother lost his pear/pair of socks.

   e) I want to by/buy those jeans.

   f) My mum got some bargains in the January sale/sail.

   g) I could tie that knot/not.

   h) Rebecca ate/eight her dinner after ate/eight.

3 Now look at the homophones you *didn't* choose in the activity above. Write a new sentence for each one.

Apply your skills

4 Complete the poem below by choosing a word from the table to fill the gaps. Each pair of lines should finish with two words that sound the same but have different meanings. Two examples are given in red.

allowed	hair	flour
flee	aloud	hare

Nonsense poem

There was a flower
Covered in _____
And a small flea
Who had to _____
And a _____
That cut its _____
I shout _____
Should this be _____?

5 Choose three words from the table above and write three sentences of your own using the words.

Check your progress

Good progress 》》
I can recognise and spell some homophones.

Excellent progress 》》
I can write using correct homophones.

Recognise silent letters

Getting you thinking

A silent letter is a letter that you cannot hear when you say the word out loud. It is only there when you write the word.

Examples: gnat, knife, write.

1 With a partner, look at the following words. They all have their first letter missing. The missing letters are silent letters. See if you can work out what the missing silent letters are.

reck

riggle

nock

nee

Now you try it

Look at the word bank below:

| rustle | climb | lamb | wreck | bomb |

2 Fill in the blank in each sentence below with a word from the word bank:

a) There was a terrible storm and there was a ship _____.

b) I heard a _____ of leaves.

c) A _____ bleated in the field.

d) The building was evacuated because there was an unexploded _____.

e) He told me he could _____ the highest mountain.

3 Each word has a silent letter – but it might not be at the start of the word. Underline the silent letter in each word.

Apply your skills

4 Unscramble the following words. Each word has a silent letter. The first one has been done for you. Then underline the silent letter in each word.

a) dwors = s<u>w</u>ord

b) rawp =

c) bumth =

d) nkkco =

5 With a partner, try and think of five different words that have silent letters.

Recognise prefixes and suffixes

Getting you thinking

A *prefix* is added to the beginning of a word.

Example: paint → repaint

A *suffix* is added to the end of a word.

Example: friend → friendless

1 With a partner, look at the following words and underline the prefixes and suffixes:

a) disagree

b) teaching

c) timeless

d) kindness

e) misunderstanding.

How does it work?

By adding a prefix to the start of a word or a suffix to the end of a word, we can change the meaning of a word.

Now you try it

Look at these prefixes:

| fore | anti | non | mis |

2 Add one of the prefixes to the words in red in the sentences below, to change the meaning of that word:

a) My teacher told me to read more _____fiction.

b) I turned the handle _____clockwise.

c) The sun isn't out today and the _____cast is for the weather to be dull.

d) My writing was good except for one _____take.

Apply your skills

Look at these suffixes:

ful	al	ness

3 Complete each of the red words with one of the suffixes.

a) He always showed me kind_____.

b) I laughed because it was such a comic_____ situation.

c) Katy was off school because she had an ill_____.

d) My best friend is always cheer_____.

e) I'm thank_____ that all my brothers and sisters are happy.

4 Write a few sentences of your own using some of the prefixes and suffixes in the tables above. Your sentences can be about your friends.

Check your progress

Good progress ⟫
I can recognise prefixes and suffixes.

Excellent progress ⟫⟫
I can use prefixes and suffixes in my own writing.

Check your progress

Good progress

- [ ] I can use the look-think-say-cover-write-check method to learn unknown spellings.
- [ ] I can recognise and spell some homophones.
- [ ] I can work out which letter in a word is the silent letter.
- [ ] I can recognise prefixes and suffixes.

Excellent progress

- [ ] I can use the look-think-say-cover-write-check method and use a dictionary to check my spelling.
- [ ] I can write using correct homophones.
- [ ] I can recognise and spell some words using silent letters.
- [ ] I can use prefixes and suffixes in my own writing.

Teacher Guide

Securing basic literacy skills is a key priority for all children so they have the essential building blocks they need to become effective learners. The *Aiming for...* series supports the development of reading and writing skills in a structured yet engaging way whilst enabling teachers to effectively track the progress their students are making.

The activities in the books start by modelling the essential skills for students. This is followed by opportunities for them to practise and then demonstrate independently what they know and can do across each reading and writing strand by applying the skills. Throughout, students are encouraged to identify where they are in their learning and what their next steps will be. Using familiar assessment for learning strategies, the teacher can also gather and review secure evidence of day-to-day progress in each strand.

The examples and activities within the reading series aim to support students to develop key decoding and comprehension skills, including using a range of strategies to read for meaning, finding information, inferring and deducing and understanding writers' use of language and structure. Within the writing series, students are encouraged not only to expand the grammatical constructions they use but also to add descriptive power to their vocabulary, resulting in more imaginative, interesting and thoughtful writing.

Building on the success of the original *Aiming for...* series, this latest edition covers the 2014 curriculum. Chapters have been updated to include coverage of the Key Stage 3 Programme of Study and the Grammar, Vocabulary and Punctuation Appendix to the Key Stage 2 Programme of Study.

At the end of each chapter, the two sets of progress statements enable students to assess themselves, deciding if they have made good or excellent progress in the session. These statements have been designed to parallel the existing national curriculum levels, where good progress demonstrates the student is working at a low/secure level 3 *within the skills addressed in the session*, and excellent progress demonstrates a secure/high level 3.

The Teacher Guide section of this latest edition has also been updated and provides essential advice on how teachers can support students to make great progress in English. Although the *Aiming for...* books are designed for students to use with a level of independence, it is particularly important that, as students are developing their skills at this earlier level, the teacher is able to assess and mediate this process as appropriate. The Teacher Guide includes additional starter activities that provide an opportunity to secure the underlying knowledge students will need in order to tackle the focused activities successfully.

Natalie Packer

Series editor

Starter 1

Making sentences: 'The sun shines on...'

Students all sit on chairs in a circle. Choose one student to stand in the middle of the circle then take away the spare chair.

The person in the middle calls: 'The sun shines on...'. Another student (selected if you wish) completes the sentence. For example

> The sun shines on...everyone who has a pet cat.

Explain to students that this is a *sentence* because it *makes sense*.

In response to the sentence, students who own a pet cat change places with one another. They cannot change places with the person sitting next to them.

While students are changing places, the caller must try to find a seat. The student left without a seat at the end becomes the next caller.

As students get into the game, they may come with ideas such as

> The sun shines on everyone who supports Liverpool.

> The sun shines on everyone wearing a watch.

> The sun shines on everyone whose first name starts with the letter 'P'.

As an extra rule, explain that students can choose to say something that doesn't make a complete sentence. In this case, everyone stays sitting down. This could be followed by some discussion about what makes a sentence make sense.

Starter 2

Unfortunately/fortunately

This is another game to reinforce understanding of what makes a sentence. Keeping students sitting in the circle, get them to take it in turns to say a sentence and build up a story beginning alternately with the words 'Unfortunately' and 'Fortunately'. For example

> Unfortunately, Lee fell into the sea.

> Fortunately, he could swim.

> Unfortunately, there were sharks in the water.

> Fortunately, there was a boat nearby.

Keep going round the circle for as long as possible. When a student gets stuck, start a new round.

Starter 3

Clap/click

This game reinforces the use of capital letters and full stops. Choose some sentences and read each one aloud twice. The second time you read the sentence, ask students to clap their hands for a capital letter and click their fingers when there should be a full stop. You could use the sentences students have come up with in the starter activities above, or use the examples below:

> Lewis Hamilton is a champion.

> Some footballers miss open goals.

My mates hang out down town.

I'm having a sleepover this weekend.

We're going to Spain this summer with my aunt and my cousins.

I have a naughty new puppy who wees all over the floor.

As an extension to this activity, you could vary the sentence types and get students to stamp one foot for a question mark and both feet for an exclamation mark. Here are some example sentences:

Do you think it will snow today?

Hey! You!

Stop at once!

Have you seen the wolf?

1 Use capital letters

Getting you thinking
When students have looked at the example sentence, ask them to explain why 'the' should have a capital letter. Then ask them why 'Football' does not need a capital letter and 'october' does, to make sure they fully understand.

How does it work?
To reinforce the point that capital letters make writing clearer, give students some further examples of incorrect uses:

mr johnson's pet Monkey escaped.

James winters loved hot Summer days.

Now you try it
Students should correct the sentences as follows:

a) My brother Joe is taller than me.

b) This Christmas will be a fun time.

c) Christina and Joanne are friends.

d) We travelled from Pembroke to Coventry on Tuesday.

Make sure they note that each sentence must *start* with a capital letter, as well as identifying the missing capitals on the proper nouns.

If students work individually on this activity, have them work in pairs afterwards and explain their choices to each other.

Apply your skills
You might wish to photocopy this extract for students to mark up rather than writing out. You could model the first sentence on the whiteboard if necessary.

They wanted to steal the key. He must hide the key and escape to Manchester. He'd catch an aeroplane to New Zealand where he'd meet Dave Groves. Dave would find him a safe house and he could stay there until October or November.

2 Explain what a sentence is and understand how to use sentences

Getting you thinking
As a reinforcement exercise, write the following sentences on the whiteboard and ask students to copy them down and underline the subject, verb and object in three different colours:

We went to see the film.

My auntie gave me fifty pounds.

The best team won the trophy.

How does it work?
For more practice, students could find verbs to go in these sentences:

Mr Rude _____ over his neighbour's plants.

Indira _____ her packed lunch.

You could also provide sentences with missing subjects and objects for students to complete to make sure they really understand how to use sentences.

Now you try it
Students should recognise that b), c), e) and g) make sense. They may come up with a variety of words to complete the sentences

in a), d) and f), but possible answers (with subject, verb and object) are:

a) My dad washed his car.

d) The sun shines on my garden.

f) He dug his way out.

Apply your skills
If necessary, provide some topic suggestions for students to write about (sports, films, games, etc.).

When students have completed Activity 3, ask them to explain the reasons for their choices of subject, object and verb to a partner.

3 Use full stops, question marks and exclamation marks

Getting you thinking
Explain that the expression you use when asking questions or making exclamations is different. For example, if you were asking, 'What was that noise?', the expression in your voice might rise at the end of the sentence but if you were exclaiming, 'he was terrified!', your voice might sound harsh throughout. Students could read the extract and see which punctuation *sounds* right for each sentence.

Explain that most sentences end in a full stop. Tell students that they can work out where the sentences end (and therefore where full stops go) because the capital letter shows a new sentence is about to start.

Now you try it
Sentence a) is a question so it needs a question mark. Sentence c) is not a

question but a command, so it needs an exclamation mark.

Once students have completed this activity, ask them to explain the reasons for their choices.

Apply your skills
You may want to try more examples with students before moving on to the three sentences in Activity 3. If necessary, model the first sentence as an example and have them work in pairs or small groups if they are struggling. They should conclude that a) needs an exclamation mark, b) needs a question mark and c) needs a full stop.

After they have completed Activity 4, get students to check their written sentences with a partner.

4 Use commas in lists

Now you try it
Sentences a) and d) need commas in the lists:

a) I bought chocolate, milk, eggs, bread and a cereal bar from the shop.

d) We will meet Nihal, Jason, Suzie and Chrissie outside the cinema.

Make sure students do not add a comma before the 'and' in the list.

Apply your skills

Make sure that students aren't just using commas here, but applying all the rules of sentences, including capital letters and full stops.

Encourage them to extend their practice by writing sentences that require question marks and exclamation marks, too.

5 Recognise speech in stories

Getting you thinking

Model the story by reading it to the group. Students should recognise that anything spoken is placed within the speech marks. They should also remember that each new speaker needs a new line.

Now you try it

You might wish to photocopy this passage or write it on the whiteboard so students can place the speech marks where appropriate. If working alone, students could show their completed work to a partner for checking. Model the first paragraph if necessary. Their final extracts should have speech marks as follows:

> *'They were pretty good,' Jim admitted, as the light went out again. 'They looked almost real.'*

Another scream echoed along the dark passageway. This time both boys jumped.

'That one sounded better,' Karl said.

'Yeah,' Jim nodded, and a cold breeze tickled his neck. 'They sounded really scared, didn't they?'

Karl didn't answer. The only sound in the tunnel was the creaking of the car along the track.

'Don't you think?' Jim said.

Karl still didn't answer.

'Karl?'

Apply your skills

Ensure that students don't just write four sentences of direct speech – they should include information about who said what (and how, if they are able) in order to distinguish speech from narrative text.

Chapter 2 Vary sentences for clarity, purpose and effect

Starter

The past/present game

Ask students to think of something that has happened in the past. Go round the group and get each student to state his or her event out loud. They might come up with statements such as

> *'I went on holiday to America.'*

> *'My baby brother was born.'*

> *'I had an accident.'*

Ask them to identify the words we use when talking about the past ('went', 'was' and 'had').

Then ask students to think of something that is happening now (avoid the future tense for the moment). They might come up with

> *'We are in an English lesson.'*

> *'We are listening to the teacher.'*

> *'My friend isn't listening.'*

Ask them to point out the words we use when talking about something that is happening *now* ('are' and 'isn't').

1 Recognise the present and the past tense in stories

Getting you thinking

Read the extract from *Cyber Shock* aloud to students, then go through it again, pointing out features that show it is written in the past tense – for example, 'His trousers *were* torn', 'I *expected*…'

Now you try it

Students should write about something that happened to them the day before, but if they find this difficult, they could instead write about something interesting that happened to them in the past. You could suggest an amusing incident or something that sticks out in their mind, such as an experience with a pet or an incident at school.

Apply your skills

For Activity 3, students should identify the following words in the present tense:

'I can see', 'He's', 'I've got to', 'I hear', 'turn', 'are', 'I'm'.

Students might need some help coming up with scenarios for someone who is in danger. If necessary, write some suggestions on the board for them to choose from. For example

> *In the sea, surrounded by sharks.*
>
> *In the jungle, facing a tiger.*
>
> *Being chased by a swarm of bees.*
>
> *Breaking a leg while snowboarding.*

Explain that they can write in the first person (as if they are in this dangerous situation themselves) or in the third person (describing someone else who is danger).

2 Switch between the present and the past tense

Getting you thinking

You might like to model the first sentence of this activity on the whiteboard – circling the word 'lived' and asking students what tense this is. They can then write down the other words in the past tense from the extract by themselves ('came', 'was', 'was').

Afterwards, get them to swap with a partner and check each other's work. Did they write down the same words?

Now you try it

The rewritten text should be as follows:

> *Deep down here by the dark water <u>lives</u> old Gollum, a small slimy creature. I don't know where he <u>comes</u> from, nor who or what he <u>is</u>. He <u>is</u> Gollum – as dark as darkness, except for two big round pale eyes in his thin face.*

When students have completed this activity, allow them to read their work to the rest of the class or group. Remind them to check

that the form of the verb agrees with the subject: '*lives* old Gollum' not '*live* old Gollum'.

To reinforce the idea of subject–verb agreement, ask them to correct the following sentences:

> She *stand* at the bus stop.
>
> It *climb* up the rock.
>
> He *walk* to work.

Encourage students to check with a partner or proofread their work to make sure they have a consistent and correct use of tense and subject–verb agreement.

Apply your skills

When students have completed their two paragraphs, get them to take turns and read them to each other in small groups to find out which their fellow students prefer and why.

Activity 5 is a variation on a 'thought tunnel' and should reinforce their understanding of the past tense. You can extend the activity by having a second round in which students whisper words in the present tense.

3 Join sentences together using conjunctions

Getting you thinking
Students should choose 'but' as the conjunction that joins the sentences in Activity 1.

Now you try it
Some of the examples in Activity 2 could be joined by more than one conjunction. Write the alternatives on the whiteboard:

a) 'and' or 'because'

b) 'so'

c) 'but' or 'so'

d) 'and' or 'so'.

You could extend this activity by giving more examples of sentences to be joined by conjunctions – or by giving students other possible conjunctions to join sentences.

Apply your skills
A possible answer for Activity 3 could be: 'so', 'and', 'because', 'so', although there may be other options that work. If students get any wrong, make sure they understand why a particular conjunction doesn't work in a certain place.

Chapter 3   Select appropriate and effective vocabulary

Starter 1

Charades
Each student writes the name of a famous person on card or paper. They fold the paper and place it in a hat or empty bin. Names can be from the past or present – they can be pop stars, sports personalities or actors.

Students are then divided into two groups – A and B. One member of group A takes a name from the hat. That student then has to say what the person does and say something about them until a member of their own group guesses who the person is.

Encourage students to use interesting adjectives and also verbs to describe how the person moves, talks or acts. Group A has one minute to guess correctly – if they do, they hold on to that piece of paper.

If group A doesn't guess the person within a minute, group B has one minute to guess correctly. Then group B has a turn to go first.

After the first round, A and B add up the cards they hold and their score is written down.

Starter 2

What do you know about me?
Each student writes down five sentences using adjectives to describe themselves. After they have secretly completed this writing, they will need to sit on chairs in a circle. They take it in turns to read out one thing about themselves until everyone in the circle has had a go. Repeat this five times, until every student has stated all five things about themselves.

Get students to work in pairs. One person explains what he or she knows about the other one. They then swap roles. Which student has remembered the most about the other?

A variation on this game has students writing five things about themselves, but some are false. When a student is picked to say what he or she knows about the other, the other student can say whether they think it is true or false. Encourage students to use interesting verbs and adjectives.

1 Choose interesting verbs

Getting you thinking
There are several alternative answers for this activity, but a good example might be

> 'I *noticed* a cake on the table. I *dashed* over and *grabbed* it. I *gobbled* it all up!'

If students are unfamiliar with words such as 'grabbed', encourage them to look them up in a dictionary.

Now you try it
If students are struggling to come up with verbs of their own, write a word bank on the whiteboard. For example

exclaimed	ambled over	attempted
grabbed	sped	flew

Apply your skills
Again, some students may find it helpful to have a bank of 'interesting' verbs to choose from:

vaulted	slid	heaved
pulled	pushed	pursued
raced		

As they are assessing each other's work in pairs, walk round the room and pick out some of the best examples of interesting verbs they have used. These can then be shared with the class to broaden their vocabulary.

2 Write using adjectives

Getting you thinking
Remind students that adjectives are *describing* words. They are essential to make writing varied and interesting.

After the discussion in pairs in Activity 1, get students to share their ideas for how to make the text more interesting as a whole class. Try to draw out the idea that adding varied adjectives will make the text more exciting and help readers picture things more clearly in their minds.

If students need help with Activity 2, suggest the following adjectives to liven up the rest of the text in the example:

outlandish	dull	bright
scrappy	big	green
smart		

Now you try it
Again, some students may find a word bank useful here. For example:

new	big	dirty
green	smart	clever
enormous	vicious	scruffy
large	old	feeble

Allow more than one possible answer. One example might be:

> There was a *big* lorry outside Mr Hill's *green* garage. Men were loading a *new* car onto a van. One man was dressed in an *old*, *scruffy* coat. A *vicious* dog snapped at his *enormous* feet. I knew *smart* Mr Hill would never allow this *dirty* man near his garage.

Apply your skills

Explain that a thesaurus is different from a dictionary – it does not give the *definition* of words. A thesaurus shows words that have the same *general* meaning, so that students can build up their vocabulary and use different words in their writing.

3 Write using adverbs

Getting you thinking

Explain that adverbs (as well as adjectives) are a key part of more sophisticated writing. You could start this topic by briefly explaining what an adverb is and asking students to suggest some, then write them on the board.

If students find Activity 1 difficult, give them some of the following examples:

slowly	kindly	harshly
quietly	quickly	angrily
speedily	annoyingly	excitedly

Now you try it

Possible answers for Activity 3 could be 'slowly', 'quickly', 'gently', but there are of course several options for each sentence. After students have completed the activity, go round the class and have them say which adverb they chose for each sentence. Write the different adverbs on the board for everyone to see – there may be some that other students hadn't considered.

Apply your skills

Students should be able to correctly change these adjectives into the adverbs a) hastily, b) icily and c) handily.

For more practice on this, you could give students more adjectives ending in 'y' to change to adverbs – ready, sleepy, squeaky, foggy, geeky, etc. Can they think of any of their own?

Chapter 4 Construct paragraphs and use cohesion within and between paragraphs

Starter 1

The rain pours…

This game is a variation on 'The sun shines on…', in which students extend the idea by saying: 'The rain pours on…because…' This time, sentences need to follow one another to build up a paragraph.

Students sit on chairs in a circle, with the teacher in the middle of the circle. The teacher begins the game and then chooses a student to continue. After that, the game moves round the circle clockwise. For example

Teacher: The rain pours on mean old Mr Cross.

Student 1: Because he keeps his money to himself.

Student 2: Because he never spends and he always saves.

Student 3: Because he's like Scrooge, the mean old man.

Once students get the idea of the game, you could always do without 'The rain pours on… ' and encourage students to link sentences together:

Teacher: An alien arrived at school one day.

Student 1: It had small eyes and a green skin.

Student 2: It came into our classroom.

Student 3: We hid under our desks.

After the game, explain to students that they have all made up a story on the same topic. They have linked their sentences together. If they wrote down all the sentences they had said, they would have made a paragraph.

Starter 2

Writing paragraphs

Put students in small groups (of about four) and give each group some small strips of paper. On the paper, ask each student to write one sentence about shopping – for example: 'You can buy size 13 trainers online but not in many shops.'

Then get students to place their sentences in an agreed logical order. Explain that they have formed a paragraph about one topic. If the sentences do not seem to follow a logical order, ask students if they can write one sentence to improve the paragraph.

1 Recognise paragraphs and topic sentences

Getting you thinking

This is a revision exercise to reinforce students' understanding of sentences and to introduce paragraphs as groups of sentences. Read the extract aloud to the class before they pair up to work out which is the topic sentence (the first one).

Now you try it

Explain to students that the first sentence is the topic sentence – it explains *why* the stone was mistaken for a ball.

Apply your skills

For Activity 3, explain to students that the topic sentence is the second one. The other sentences tell us where the rats had invaded and how people felt about them.

Activity 4 will test whether students can write using a topic and supporting sentences. Help them come up with some ideas for their paragraph if necessary.

2 Use supporting sentences

Getting you thinking

You may wish to show students supporting sentences, using examples from other stories, before they work on Activity 1.

How does it work?

Explain that topic sentences tell readers what the paragraph will be about. Supporting sentences expand on this by telling the reader more about the topic of the paragraph.

Now you try it

Students should pick out the first sentence as the topic sentence and realise the others are the supporting sentences.

Apply your skills

Encourage students to write imaginatively about the three pictures. If they're struggling, allow them to join up in pairs to talk about the pictures before they begin writing.

After the work on this topic, ask students to write a paragraph about a sport of their choice. They can swap books with a partner and highlight the different sentences in different colour pens/highlighters. They will need three different colour pens/highlighters for this activity.

3 Arrange paragraphs so a story makes sense

Getting you thinking
Students should work out that the order is D, B, A, C.

You may wish to photocopy the paragraphs about Cousin Mike and allow students to cut them out and place them in the right order.

Now you try it
These questions can be answered individually or in pairs or small groups. They should find the following answers:

a) The first sentence in each paragraph is the topic sentence.

b) D introduces and describes Cousin Mike; B gives more information about how horrible cousin Mike is; A explains how the writer found some spiders and used them to get his own back on Mike; C is about what happened when Mike saw the spiders.

c) The order they give information in their writing is essential in helping the reader make sense of it.

Apply your skills
For Activity 3, students should work out that the second paragraph should begin at 'We were doing fine…' and the third at 'A big wave…'.

Make sure students understand why this is by pointing out the three distinct topics. Ask them to identify the topic sentence in each paragraph.

The story about the shipwreck is unfinished. As an extension activity, students could finish the story by adding a paragraph of their own. Ask them to imagine what happened next. Get them to explore ideas orally before they write, discussing what each sentence will be about and making sure they understand the story before they write their paragraph.

To reinforce learning about paragraphs, students could storyboard the four paragraphs about Cousin Mike so the logic of the order is crystal clear in their minds. They could then storyboard the paragraphs about the shipwreck, including their own paragraph.

Chapter 5 Organise and present whole texts effectively, sequencing and structuring information, ideas and events

Starter 1

Can you do this?
Sitting at their desks, tell students to hold their left hand in the air, pointing their fingers forward and drawing a circle in the air. They then drop their left hand, raise their right hand and draw a cross in the air. Now ask them to do the two things at the same time. Teachers beware: the game may be noisy! This game shows students that it's easier to do one thing at a time. Explain that in the same way, it's easier for readers to read one thing/idea at a time, so their writing needs to be well structured and organised.

Starter 2

Ordering objects
Put nine or ten random objects on your desk. These could be, for example, a pencil, picture, football scarf, pen, photograph, cricket ball, book, painting, tennis racket. Ask students to put them in a logical order. What reasons can they give for their choice of order? Are there any items that don't seem to fit?

Story words

Write the following words on the board:

> aeroplane, computer, troll, elves, castle, rampart, gym, sword, machine gun, giant, armour, magic, knight, wolf, forest, school, car, rabbit, crown, dragon, hat, screen, internet, iPod, rap music.

Ask students to choose the ten words from this selection that they think are the most appropriate for a fairy tale. Which ten are most appropriate for a modern story?

1 Plan your writing

Getting you thinking

Students should recognise that Anita's plan is a good one, but encourage them to think of some additional points that might help to improve it. Would any sections benefit from being in a different order? What information could be added?

How does it work?

Show students Anita's plan (perhaps on the whiteboard) and talk them through each stage. Explain that they are going to need a similar plan for the next activity.

Now you try it

Explain to students that to plan and deliver an effective speech it is useful if it is about something they are interested in and enthusiastic about. Allow them to talk together in pairs or small groups first to draw out some ideas.

Get them to research the subject further. Help them to find appropriate websites or books in the library, or bring a selection of books into class.

Apply your skills

To help students prepare for writing and delivering their full speeches, model this opening to Anita's speech:

> I had always wanted a puppy but Mum said it would chew everything. She also wanted to know who'd take it for walks. I told her that she need not worry. I'd use my paper-round money to get a puppy properly trained.

Point out that Anita has settled on a quick opening, so that she could get into her subject and engage her classmates' interest. She describes how she overcame her mum's worries and persuaded her that she could look after a puppy. Anita is now ready to go on to the next part of her speech.

Get them first to write the opening for their speech and try it out with a partner, who can then suggest how it could be improved.

After students have given their speeches, pair them up again to talk about how useful a plan is in helping to organise their writing. Would they change anything if they had the chance to plan their speech again?

2 Use bullet points and headings

Getting you thinking

Students should understand that the second text (about the grey squirrel) is easier to read because the text is presented in smaller chunks.

Ask them a few questions to check their understanding:

> What are squirrel babies called?
>
> Are kittens born with their eyes closed?
>
> Can grey squirrels swim?
>
> What other colour can a grey squirrel be?

How does it work

Explain that the fact sheet on the grey squirrel works because the facts are presented clearly and in a logical order. Using bullet points allows the reader to take in the facts more easily.

Now you try it

When planning, students may wish to use bullet points, a spider diagram, note form or a flow chart. They may also wish to reorder once they have all the information they require, so this could be an opportunity to use their IT skills.

Apply your skills

Read students the fact sheet on wildcats and make sure they have understood it before they begin writing their own. You could ask questions (written or oral) to check their understanding:

Where do wildcats live?

Do wildcats hunt in groups?

Where are wildcat kittens born?

How do wildcats defend themselves?

What do wildcats look like?

Why are so few wildcats left in the wild?

3 Write the opening of a story

Getting you thinking

Explain that an engaging opening is key to grabbing and holding a reader's interest.

Read the two story openings to the class and point out the use of short sentences and interesting nouns and adjectives can help to make a good opening to a story.

There is no 'right' answer to Activity 1, but students should be able to explain why they have chosen a particular opening, giving examples of what grabbed their attention.

Now you try it

Students could work in pairs for this activity. When they have identified the features together, go through both extracts with the whole class and make sure they have spotted everything. They may need help in identifying and picking out the words or phrases that establish the setting.

4 Continue your story by describing and then solving the problem

How does it work?

Ask students to think of any stories they have read, or films they have seen, that are based on a problem that needs to be solved. Perhaps someone has been kidnapped or killed, or has witnessed a bank robbery. Perhaps a girl loves a boy but does not know if he feels the same about her…

Explain that most books and films deal with a problem that needs solving or a conflict that needs resolving. That's what makes them interesting and dramatic.

Now you try it

Encourage students to use their imaginations when considering what might happen next. What might be the problem for Kade? Finding the target? Capturing the target? Making sure the target stays alive, so Kade can get him back to prison?

Apply your skills

Check that students use sentences, paragraphs and interesting adjectives when writing the additional parts of their own stories.

Starter 1

Catch a story

The class will need a ball or a beanbag. Students should sit in a circle. You start a story and throw the beanbag. The student who catches the beanbag continues the story. Those who are shy or nervous may not catch the beanbag to join in so to get everyone to participate, tell the group that the same person cannot catch the beanbag twice.

Part of this exercise is to show students how to make up exciting stories orally.

For example

> You: A wolf was seen heading for our school.
>
> Laura: The wolf howled at the back door.
>
> Elliott: We were scared it might get in.
>
> Kermal: It had sharp claws and big yellow teeth.

If you feel the story is stagnating, end it and start a new one.

Starter 2

Something different: observation

Place chairs in a circle and allow students to observe one another for a few minutes. A volunteer leaves the room. Out of the room, the student changes something about themselves, such as his or her hairstyle, taking off a tie, undoing shoelaces or exchanging shoes for trainers.

When the volunteer comes back, students have to spot the difference. The student who spots it first has a go at being different.

Explain to students that to write well, they need to be observant.

1 Recognise different text types

Getting you thinking

Students should work out that the example in Activity 1 is from a story (fiction). You could go further and draw out the genre of the story (horror or mystery). Which words reveal a) that this is fiction and b) what its genre is?

Now you try it

Students should reach the conclusion that

a) is descriptive (diary)

b) is informative (letter of complaint)

c) is persuasive (an advert/brochure)

d) is instructive (manual).

Apply your skills

You might wish to go through the key features of a text at a basic level before students begin writing these two pieces:

* **Descriptive** – to describe something and present thoughts and feelings about an event or a place (fiction).

* **Informative** – to write about something personal (diary) or to write a newspaper article about something factual (non-fiction).

* **Instructive** – to present information in a logical order, for example what to do in a hotel in case of an emergency (non-fiction).

* **Persuasive** – to make you want to buy or do something. Often important words are repeated, part of the text might be in capitals and exclamation marks are used (non-fiction).

2 Write for reader and purpose

Getting you thinking
Explain in simple terms the basics of formality and informality in writing. When writing to a friend, for example, students would use informal words and phrases (see if they can come up with some examples and write them on the board). When writing to an adult or someone they don't know, they would use more formal (polite and official) words and phrases. This time ask them to come up with examples of scenarios in which they might use formal expressions.

Apply your skills
It might be worth pointing out that friendly letters can have a variety of sign-offs, such as 'Cheers', 'See you soon', 'Love' and 'Best wishes'. A formal letter would end 'Yours sincerely' if it began with 'Dear Mr or Mrs'. It would end 'Yours faithfully' if it began with 'Dear Sir or Madam'.

When writing to an adult Lissie might be more formal, especially as she wishes to persuade Isabella's mum about the party. She might write 'Dear Mrs Morgan' and the sign-off would be, 'Yours sincerely'.

Chapter 7 Write imaginative, interesting and thoughtful texts

Starter

Random words
To build up students' vocabulary and encourage concentration, play the random word game. All you need for this is a children's fiction book. Ask students for a number between 1 and 50, then turn to that page. Now ask for a number from 1 to 30. This gives you the line. Now ask for a number from 1 to 10. This gives you the word.

Write the selected word on the board. Ask if anyone can define it. (You may need to use your discretion about whether the selected word is too easy or too hard.)

Play the game six times so you have six words written down. See if the students can make a sentence using the six words. They can add pronouns and conjunctions if necessary.

If students find the exercise a struggle, choose your own six words. For example

seaside	holiday	we
near	are	on

This becomes: 'We are on holiday near the seaside.' Or: 'We are near the seaside, on holiday'.

1 Express opinions

Getting you thinking
Allow students to express their own opinions concerning pop stars and/or bands. They may want to talk about the choices students of their own age have made in the examples.

Now you try it
Students could make a short presentation to the group or class about their favourite band or singer. They might need help to research some facts, so guide them to appropriate magazines or websites. Remind them to write their information down as bullet points.

Allow students to write down their choices and narrow the final down to the top three choices. Then allow them to vote for the overall winner. Explain that they have expressed an opinion – this means that other groups or classes might disagree with the result.

Apply your skills
Students might find a writing frame useful for this activity.

For example

My favourite sports person is...

(s)he participated in the...on Saturday.

...was lucky to...

My sports star attended...

...won/ran/scored...when....

My sports person could...if they...

(You may need to adapt the words, depending upon the sport their personality is involved in.)

As an extension to this activity, ask students to research and write about another person who they think should be sports person of the year. Read out their choices and allow the class to vote. The winner is the personality who receives the most votes.

2 Redraft your text to improve it

Getting you thinking
Draw out from students how the text could be improved – for example, by giving more information about the different forms bullying can take, the various people students might approach for help or how bullies are dealt with or give examples for the final sentence.

Apply your skills
Get some students to read out their redrafted text. Others can then suggest further improvements to the original draft.

Chapter 8   Use correct spelling

Starter 1

Hangman
This classic game can be played on the whiteboard. Give students a general theme, such as 'hobbies' or 'things you might find in a classroom'. Allow students to select a word related to that theme and put in dashes that match with the number of letters in the word. For example, a six-letter word should have six dashes on the board.

The group needs to guess a letter, one at a time. (Explain what vowels are, if necessary, and show them that it is best to use vowels for their first few guesses.)

A correctly guessed letter goes above the dash. A letter that does not make up the word is recorded and the hangman's gibbet is started.

Starter 2

The blending game
Divide the group in two: A and B. Stick labels with the beginnings of words on the group A students' backs.

Stick the endings of words on the backs of the other half (group B). Each student has to find a matching partner to make up a complete word.

Here are some suggestions using 'est':

Ch – est	B – est
T – est	L – est
W – est	R – est
V – est	P – est

You can also use 'ock':

Cl – ock	R – ock
Sh – ock	Bl – ock
T – ock	D – ock
S – ock	Fl – ock.

You can also use 'ap':

Ch – ap	Cl – ap
C – ap	Scr – ap
R – ap	M – ap

Mixing the endings can vary the game:

Ch – est

Ch – ap = Chest/tap or chap/test

Turning singular to plural
Point out to students that singular words can become plural by adding an 's' to the word:

Apple – Apple<u>s</u>	Hand – Hand<u>s</u>
Finger – Finger<u>s</u>	Plum – Plum<u>s</u>
Thumb – Thumb<u>s</u>	Desk – Desk<u>s</u>

Point out that for some words that end in an 'x', students need to add an 'es'.

Fox – Fox<u>es</u>   Box – Box<u>es</u>

An 'es' is added for words ending in 'sh':

Bush – Bush<u>es</u>

Flush – Flush<u>es</u>

Dish – Dish<u>es</u>

Words that end in 'ch' also need an 'es':

Lunch – Lunch<u>es</u>

Munch – Munch<u>es</u>

Punch – Punch<u>es</u>

A further variation of the blending game
Group A can be the singular words and group B can be the plurals.

Half of group B can wear 's'; the other half can wear 'es'. Then A and B can swap.

1 Use different methods for spelling

Getting you thinking
Model the 'look-say-think-cover-write-check' method by demonstrating the process. Then allow students to practise. Explain that in the 'look' stage, they should think about how to break the word into smaller pieces or syllables – do any of the smaller bits remind them of patterns of letters from other words?

Parts of the word that might cause problems include double letters or a vowel that isn't pronounced as you would expect.

When checking, if they got the word wrong in the 'write' stage, ask them to look carefully at where they went wrong and then to try again.

How does it work?
As an extra tip, explain to the students that whenever they have to copy a new word from the board, from a book or from a dictionary, they should try to write the whole word in one go rather than keep looking back after every few letters.

Apply your skills
Students may need more direction with this activity. Help them by modelling how to do this with a CCVC (consonant-consonant-vowel-consonant) word such as 'swim':

* Get them to sound out the word to their partner first. The sound should give them a clue to the first two letters (sw).

- Find the letter 's' in the dictionary.
- When they have found 's', scan down the page for words beginning 'sw'.

- Then look up the third letter ('i')…they should find it from there!

2 Recognise homophones

Getting you thinking
Homophones are one of the most common causes of spelling errors, so make sure students fully understand the importance of checking spelling in a dictionary if they're not sure. If they use word-processing programs, warn them that the spellcheck won't pick up errors like this!

Apply your skills
Students should recognise the missing words are: flour, flee, hare, hair, aloud, allowed.

3 Recognise silent letters

Getting you thinking
Students should work out the silent letters are w, k, w, k.

Now you try it
Students should have the following answers:

a) wreck

b) rustle

c) lamb

d) bomb

e) climb

Apply your skills
Students could work in pairs on Activity 4. They should have the following;

b) rawp = wrap

c) bumth = thumb

d) nkkco= knock

4 Recognise prefixes and suffixes

Getting you thinking
Students should work out the following answers:

a) disagree

b) teaching

c) timeless

d) kindness

e) misunderstanding

Now you try it
Students should have the following answers:

a) non

b) anti

c) fore

d) mis

Apply your skills
Students should have the following answers:

a) ness

b) al

c) ness

d) ful

e) ful

For those who find this work challenging, you might wish to present them with a list of prefixes and suffixes.

Notes

Notes